PRAYERS AT MEALS

Michael Kwatera, O.S.B.

and Dietrich Reinhart, O.S.B.

The Liturgical Press
Collegeville, Minnesota

Nihil obstat: Robert C. Harren, J.C.L., *Censor deputatus.*
Imprimatur: + George H. Speltz, Bishop of St. Cloud, May 24, 1983.
Copyright © 1983 by The Order of St. Benedict, Inc., Collegeville, Minnesota.
Printed in the United States of America.
ISBN 0-8146-1318-7

Michael Kwatera, O.S.B., and Dietrich Reinhart, O.S.B., are monks of St. John's Abbey, Collegeville, Minnesota.

ABOUT THE COVER: The photo of a woodcarving by Br. Placid Stuckenschneider, O.S.B., is in reference to Jesus feeding the multitudes. For centuries artists have used this Eucharistic symbol of loaves, fish, and a basket in portraying scenes of the Last Supper. The woodcarving decorates a wall of the guest dining room of St. John's Abbey and University.

Dedicated to our parents,
in whose homes we first learned to pray at meals,
and to our monastic family at Saint John's Abbey,
who still teach and encourage us to pray.

CONTENTS

FOREWORD

Like the good Italian patriarch that he was, Saint Benedict (c.480–c.547) knew that the dinner table is a sacred place for families to gather. That is why he included many helpful directions for community meals in his *Rule* for monks; for example, he insisted that everyone "come to table before the verse so that all may say the verse and pray and sit down at table together" (43:13, *RB 1980: The Rule of St. Benedict* [Collegeville: The Liturgical Press, 1981], 245). Benedict knew that it isn't always easy to get the family rounded up before the food gets cold (even if they are hungry), and he believed that prayer should nourish the spirit before food nourishes the body.

Prayers before and after meals are part of the ancient tradition of Jewish and Christian worship that each generation of believers must make its own. They help dedicate the day to God just as morning and evening prayers do; indeed, busy families may find that meals provide the best (or only) opportunities for prayer together.

The prayers in this book were written a decade ago and, after falling on the ears of our brethren at Saint John's Abbey for a good long while, have been revised to reflect deepening experience of the Church's liturgical year. The heart of each season's prayers is a common introduction and response, drawn from Scripture, expressive of that season's central meaning and, thus, proclaimed from day to day. A variety of opening words, blessings and thanksgivings – based on Scripture as well – surround each season's core and disclose the richness hidden in these all too familiar words. Those who use these prayers will hear echoes of the Scripture readings proclaimed at the Sunday and weekday Eucharist and thereby continue to be formed by the Word of God.

In several prayers, the leader is invited to include the names of particular persons (those who prepared the meal, family members who are ill), but this might be done wherever the sense of the text encourages it. The inclusion of the names of loved ones will make these prayers more personal.

Blessings upon your table and upon all who taste there the Lord's spiritual and bodily nourishment!

Dietrich Reinhart, O.S.B.
Michael Kwatera, O.S.B.

Advent

These prayers are used from the Saturday preceding the First Sunday of Advent through Christmas Eve. They could be included in the ceremony of lighting the Advent wreath.

PRAYER

BEFORE THE MEAL

Leader   Just as the rain and snow
come down from heaven,
giving seed for sowing and bread to eat,
so shall the word be
that goes forth from the mouth of God.
A voice cries:
"Prepare in the wilderness a way for the Lord.
Clear a highway across the desert for our God."

ALL   Every valley shall be lifted up,
every mountain and hill brought low.

Leader   Sow freely, Lord God, the seed of your blessing
upon our table and upon all of us.
May it strengthen us to serve you
and each other.
This we ask through Christ our Lord.

ALL   Amen.

AFTER THE MEAL

Leader   Lord our God,
we thank you for this meal together
and for inviting us to accept your kingdom
like children taking bread
from the hand of their parents.
Let us live in your peace,
at home with you all the days of our lives.
We ask this through Christ our Lord.

ALL   Amen.

BEFORE THE MEAL

Leader   The victory of the Lord is near,
already it is close,
his salvation shall not be delayed.
A voice cries:
"Prepare in the wilderness a way for the Lord.
Clear a highway across the desert for our God."

ALL   Every valley shall be lifted up,
every mountain and hill brought low.

Leader   All-powerful God,
look kindly on us,
bless this table
and unite us to all people everywhere
who wait for the coming of your Son.
We ask this through Christ our Lord.

ALL   Amen.

AFTER THE MEAL

Leader   We thank you, Giver of all good gifts,
for the grace of life renewed,
the strength of life together
and the promise of life to come,
through Christ our Lord.

ALL   Amen.

PRAYER **3**

Leader   The Savior does not call out
or lift his voice high,
nor does he make himself heard
in the open streets.
But a voice comes before him saying:
"Prepare in the wilderness a way for the Lord.
Clear a highway across the desert for our God."

ALL   Every valley shall be lifted up,
every mountain and hill brought low.

Leader   Lord, bless the food we are about to eat
and bless the cooks *(name them)*
who have labored to prepare it.
Make us all a sign of the One who is to come.
We make this prayer in his name,
both now and for ever.

ALL   Amen.

AFTER THE MEAL

Leader   Give us grateful hearts, our Father,
for all your mercies
and grant us the grace to love others
as fully as you have loved us,
through Christ our Lord.

ALL   Amen.

PRAYER **4**

BEFORE THE MEAL

Leader   The Lord God is our refuge and strength,
a helper close at hand in times of distress.
A voice cries:
"Prepare in the wilderness a way for the Lord.
Clear a highway across the desert for our God."

ALL   Every valley shall be lifted up,
every mountain and hill brought low.

Leader   Lord God,
bless this table
and let the food we share
strengthen us in your service.
We ask this through the One
who comes in your name,
and keeps us safe,
for ever and ever.

ALL   Amen.

AFTER THE MEAL

Leader   God of mercy,
we thank you for showing us your goodness
and loving kindness at this meal,
and we ask the same blessings
for all the members of your family,
through Christ our Lord.

ALL   Amen.

Christmas

These prayers are used from Christmas Day through the Feast of the Baptism of the Lord.

BEFORE THE MEAL

Leader   Lord,
you have made our gladness greater,
you have made our joy increase.
For you are called:
Wonder-Counsellor, Mighty-God,
Eternal-Father, the Prince-of-Peace.

ALL   Unto us a child is born,
unto us a son is given. Alleluia!

Leader   Lord our God,
bless this food we are about to eat
and look kindly upon
those who have prepared it:
(name them).
We ask this through your Son,
who out of the wonder of your love
lives in our midst,
now and for ever.

ALL   Amen.

AFTER THE MEAL

Leader   We thank you, Lord God,
for the wonders you work –
for food and friendship in your house.
Above all,
we thank you for the gift of your Son,
who is one with us
both now and for ever.

ALL   Amen.

PRAYER 2

Leader Dwellers in a land dark as death,
we have seen a great light.
The Lord in his radiance
shines upon us.
And this is the name we give him:
Wonder-Counsellor, Mighty-God,
Eternal-Father, the Prince-of-Peace.

ALL Unto us a child is born,
unto us a son is given. Alleluia!

Leader Mighty God,
visit this table
and renew the strength and vision of us all.
Bless this time together,
through Christ our Lord.

ALL Amen.

AFTER THE MEAL

Leader Mighty God,
we thank you for looking upon us in our need.
Help us bend our strength
day by day
toward serving your people,
through Christ our Lord.

ALL Amen.

BEFORE THE MEAL

Leader   O God, we ponder your love
within your house.
Your praise, like your name,
reaches the ends of the earth.
For you are called:
Wonder-Counsellor, Mighty-God,
Eternal-Father, the Prince-of-Peace.

ALL   Unto us a child is born,
unto us a son is given. Alleluia!

Leader   Eternal Father,
we praise and bless you
for the constant goodness you show us.
Be with us at this meal
as we celebrate
the fulfillment of your promise
in the coming of your Son,
Jesus Christ, our Lord.

ALL   Amen.

AFTER THE MEAL

Leader   Eternal Father,
accept our thanksgiving
for bringing us together
to share this meal.
Keep us as faithful witnesses
to the joy which is ours
in the gift of your Son.
We ask this in his name.

ALL   Amen.

PRAYER 4

BEFORE THE MEAL

Leader Listen to what the Lord God has to say –
a voice that speaks of peace
for his people and his friends.
He is called:
Wonder-Counsellor, Mighty-God,
Eternal-Father, the Prince-of-Peace.

ALL Unto us a child is born,
unto us a son is given. Alleluia!

Leader God of harmony and peace,
bless us
as we enjoy the gifts
you have given us.
May our eating together
be a sign of the peace and goodness
you give to all people
in your Son, Jesus Christ.

ALL Amen.

AFTER THE MEAL

Leader Lord Jesus,
you are the Prince of Peace.
We rejoice that you have begun your reign
and give thanks to you,
great gift from on high,
in the fullness of the Spirit,
both now and for ever.

ALL Amen.

Ordinary Time I

These prayers are used during the weeks following the Feast of the Baptism of the Lord until Ash Wednesday.

PRASER 1

BEFORE THE MEAL

Leader   Everlasting God,
Maker of the wide world,
you never grow weary
of those you have created.
Everything waits for you full of hope,
all the living ask you for food.

ALL   You open your hand, always in time,
and sustain our every moment.

Leader   Creator of all,
in your kindness, bless this food.
Give us strength
and bring us anew
to the task of building your kingdom.
We ask this through Christ our Lord.

ALL   Amen.

AFTER THE MEAL

Leader   We thank you, our Lord and Maker,
for the gift of food
and rejoice in the daily call to serve you.
To you be praise,
both now and for ever.

ALL   Amen.

PRAYER **2**

BEFORE THE MEAL

Leader   Lord, our God,
all is yours in heaven and on earth.
Everything waits for you full of hope,
all the living ask you for food.

    ALL   You open your hand, always in time,
and sustain our every moment.

Leader   Lord,
bless our table
and make it a sign
of our belonging to you and to each other,
through Christ our Lord.

    ALL   Amen.

AFTER THE MEAL

Leader   Lord,
we thank you for the bountiful love
you show to those who share our table
and to all those dear to us,
through your Son Jesus,
who abides with us,
both now and for ever.

    ALL   Amen.

PRAYER 3

BEFORE THE MEAL

Leader   Lord,
we commit ourselves to you,
trusting in your great love.
Everything waits for you full of hope,
all the living ask you for food.

ALL   You open your hand, always in time,
and sustain our every moment.

Leader   Lord,
bless our family through this meal
and renew the energies we use in your service.
We ask this in the name of Jesus Christ,
in whom all things hold together,
for ever and ever.

ALL   Amen.

AFTER THE MEAL

Leader   Father,
we thank you for this food
and all the daily reminders
of your care for this house.
To you, Guardian of all,
be honor and glory,
both now and for ever.

ALL   Amen.

PRAYER **4**

BEFORE THE MEAL

Leader   Lord,
the world around us comes from you,
provided for us out of love.
Everything waits for you full of hope,
all the living ask you for food.

ALL   You open your hand, always in time,
and sustain our every moment.

Leader   Lord,
bless this food
you have given us in your love.
Renew us in mind and body
as we share this meal,
through Christ our Lord.

ALL   Amen.

AFTER THE MEAL

Leader   Lord,
we thank you for the food
that strengthens us
and empowers us to share your gifts with others,
as did your Son Jesus,
who loves us
both now and for ever.

ALL   Amen.

Lent

These prayers are used from Ash Wednesday through Wednesday of Holy Week.

BEFORE THE MEAL

Leader   We have sinned against the Lord, our God,
and can only wait in prayer and fasting
for a time of favor.
Let us be confident.
Though our sins are like scarlet,
they shall be white as snow.

ALL   Though they are red as crimson,
they shall be made like wool.

Leader   God of our ancestors,
may our time of prayer and fasting
open us to your work of forgiveness
and free us to rejoice
in the sacrifice of your Son,
Jesus Christ, our Lord.

ALL   Amen.

AFTER THE MEAL

Leader   Lord God,
we wait for you to bring down our strongholds
and break the hold of sin in our lives.
We thank you
for nourishing us as we wait
and preparing us for the new life to come,
through Christ our Lord.

ALL   Amen.

PRAYER **2**

BEFORE THE MEAL

Leader   We have stumbled in our sinful ways,
as if we could not be healed.
Let us return to the Lord, our God.
Though our sins are like scarlet,
they shall be white as snow.

ALL   Though they are red as crimson,
they shall be made like wool.

Leader   God of mercy,
uncover your face
and be gracious to us.
Heal us
and out of your own bounty
give us new life,
through Christ our Lord.

ALL   Amen.

AFTER THE MEAL

Leader   Merciful God,
we thank you for your kindness
which exceeds all we ever knew of you.
To you, Healer of us all,
be honor and glory,
both now and for ever.

ALL   Amen.

PRAYER **3**

Leader   Now is the time to lay down fear
and purify our love through serving others.
Though our sins are like scarlet,
they shall be white as snow.

ALL   Though they are red as crimson,
they shall be made like wool.

Leader   God, holy and strong,
bless this food
and give us strength
to bring your love
to those in suffering and pain
(especially _____*).*
We ask this through Christ our Lord.

ALL   Amen.

AFTER THE MEAL

Leader   We thank you, Lord, for calling us,
for nourishing us
that we might sacrifice ourselves.
To you, God of the poor and the lowly,
we pledge our strength,
both now and for ever.

ALL   Amen.

PRAYER 4

BEFORE THE MEAL

Leader   Let us turn back to the Lord, our God;
for he is gracious and compassionate,
long-suffering and ever constant,
always ready to relent.
Though our sins are like scarlet,
they shall be white as snow.

ALL   Though they are red as crimson,
they shall be made like wool.

Leader   Ever-patient God,
meet us as we set ourselves to know you
and leave a blessing upon our table
and all those dear to us.
We ask this through Christ our Lord.

ALL   Amen.

AFTER THE MEAL

Leader   Abiding Lord,
we thank you for this meal
and for your faithful presence in our lives.
As we grow more deeply open to you,
we shall praise and magnify your name,
for ever and ever.

ALL   Amen.

Easter Triduum

The Easter triduum is a three-day celebration of the Lord's death and resurrection. It begins on Holy Thursday "with the evening Mass of the Lord's Supper, reaches its high point in the Easter vigil, and closes with evening prayer on Easter Sunday" (Roman Calendar, no. 19).

The following prayers are used on the most holy days of the Lord's passion, death, and resurrection.

HOLY THURSDAY

BEFORE THE MEAL

Leader   Christ for our sake
became obedient unto death.
Let us worship him and say:
We adore you, O Christ, and we praise you.

ALL   Because by your holy cross
you have redeemed the world.

Leader   Lord Jesus,
be with us as we share this meal.
Prepare us to celebrate with faith
the saving deeds you have worked for us,
and let us share in your passing-over
from death to life,
both now and for ever.

ALL   Amen.

AFTER THE MEAL

Leader   Glory and praise to you,
Lord Jesus Christ,
for sharing yourself with your apostles
at the Last Supper
and for giving your love to us
at this meal.
Give us grateful hearts
for the life you poured out for us,
for the suffering that takes our sin away.
Glory and praise to you, Lord,
both now and for ever.

ALL   Amen.

BEFORE THE MEAL

Leader   Christ for our sake
became obedient unto death,
even to death on a cross.
Let us worship him and say:
We adore you, O Christ, and we praise you.

ALL   Because by your holy cross
you have redeemed the world.

Leader   Lord Jesus,
it is right that we should glory in your cross,
for you bring us life, salvation, and resurrection.
Draw us closer to you at this table,
and let us share in your passing-over
from death to life,
both now and for ever.

ALL   Amen.

AFTER THE MEAL

Leader   Glory and praise to you,
Lord Jesus Christ,
for dying on the cross
so that all might receive the life
that never ends.
Give us grateful hearts
for the life you poured out for us,
for the suffering that takes our sin away.
Glory and praise to you, Lord,
both now and for ever.

ALL   Amen.

HOLY SATURDAY

BEFORE THE MEAL

Leader   Christ for our sake
became obedient unto death,
even death on a cross.
Therefore God has exalted him
and given him the name above every name.
Let us worship him and say:
We adore you, O Christ, and we praise you.

ALL   Because by your holy cross
you have redeemed the world.

Leader   Lord Jesus, victor over death,
fill this time together with your blessing.
Remove the sadness that sin places in our hearts,
and let us share the joy of your passing over
from death to life,
both now and for ever.

ALL   Amen.

AFTER THE MEAL

Leader   Glory and praise to you,
Lord Jesus Christ,
for making holy the graves of all believers
and for giving joy to those who have died.
Give us grateful hearts
for the life you poured out for us,
for the suffering that takes our sin away.
Glory and praise to you, Lord,
both now and for ever.

ALL   Amen.

BEFORE THE MEAL

Leader   This is the day the Lord has made.
Let us rejoice and be glad,
let us praise the Lord for his goodness.
For behold, Jesus died
and now lives for evermore. Alleluia!

ALL   He has gone before us.
Yet he is with us for all time. Alleluia!

Leader   Lord,
on this most holy day
let your blessing rest upon us
and upon our table.
Strengthen us in this time together.
We ask this in Jesus' name.

ALL   Amen.

AFTER THE MEAL

Leader   Blest are you, Lord our God,
who gather us together in Jesus' name.
We thank you for sharing your life with us,
both in this meal
and in all the ways you sustain us,
through Christ, our Risen Lord.

ALL   Amen.

Easter Season I

These prayers are used from Easter Monday until Ascension Thursday.

PRAYER 1

BEFORE THE MEAL

Leader　This is the day the Lord has made.
　　　　Let us rejoice and be glad,
　　　　let us praise the Lord for his goodness.
　　　　For behold, Jesus died
　　　　and now lives for evermore. Alleluia!

　ALL　He has gone before us.
　　　　Yet he is with us for all time. Alleluia!

Leader　Lord,
　　　　in this most holy season
　　　　let your blessing rest upon us
　　　　and upon our table.
　　　　Strengthen us in this time together.
　　　　We ask this in Jesus' name.

　ALL　Amen.

AFTER THE MEAL

Leader　Blest are you, Lord our God,
　　　　who gather us together in Jesus' name.
　　　　We thank you for sharing your life with us,
　　　　both in this meal
　　　　and in all the ways you sustain us,
　　　　through Christ, our Risen Lord.

　ALL　Amen.

PRAYER 2

BEFORE THE MEAL

Leader   We have cause for abiding joy;
for God raised Jesus up
and set him free from the grip of death.
Behold, Jesus died
and now lives for evermore. Alleluia!

ALL   He has gone before us.
Yet he is with us for all time. Alleluia!

Leader   Father,
bless this food and this time together.
Strengthen us
to live together in love,
united to Jesus
whom you have made both Lord and Christ,
for ever and ever.

ALL   Amen.

AFTER THE MEAL

Leader   Father,
we thank you for this meal
and all that comes to us
through your beloved Son,
who is truly risen from the grave,
for ever and ever.

ALL   Amen.

PRAYER 3

BEFORE THE MEAL

Leader   The Father has given us
birth into a living hope
that nothing can destroy
or spoil or wither.
For behold, Jesus died
and now lives for evermore. Alleluia!

ALL   He has gone before us.
Yet he is with us for all time. Alleluia!

Leader   Ever-merciful God,
bless this table,
and nurture our faith
'til it grows into
praise, glory and honor
at the revelation of Christ Jesus,
our Lord.

ALL   Amen.

AFTER THE MEAL

Leader   Upholder of all,
we put our faith in you,
and thank you for keeping us safe,
protecting us by your power
until salvation is revealed
at the end of time
in Christ Jesus, our Lord.

ALL   Amen.

PRAYER 4

Leader   The Father has found us in our brokenness
and in his divine mercy
has made us whole
in the body of his Son.
Behold, Jesus died
and now lives for evermore. Alleluia!

ALL   He has gone before us.
Yet he is with us for all time. Alleluia!

Leader   God who reconciles,
bless the food we are about to eat,
and let this meal together
be a sign of the unity
we share for all time
in the body of our risen Savior,
Jesus Christ, the Lord.

ALL   Amen.

AFTER THE MEAL

Leader   We thank you, the one Lord,
for nourishing this family
and molding us into a holy people.
United in Jesus Christ,
risen from the dead,
we give you praise
both now and for ever.

ALL   Amen.

Easter Season II

These prayers are used from Ascension Thursday through Pentecost Sunday.

PRAYER 1

BEFORE THE MEAL

Leader   The Lord Jesus has not forsaken us.
He will come back,
glorious in the love of his Father.
For behold, Jesus died
and now lives with the Father for evermore. Alleluia!

ALL   He has gone before us.
Yet he is with us for all time. Alleluia!

Leader   Lord Jesus,
send your Spirit
to bless this table.
Give us joy in knowing the love
in which we live and move
and have our being,
for ever and ever.

ALL   Amen.

AFTER THE MEAL

Leader   Lord Jesus,
because you live
we too have life in abundance
and have come to know the Father.
To you, Lord of all,
be honor and glory
both now and for ever.

ALL   Amen.

PRAYER **2**

BEFORE THE MEAL

Leader　　The Lord has ascended on high,
and now our life
lies hidden with him in God.
Behold, Jesus died
and now lives with the Father for evermore. Alleluia!

ALL　　He has gone before us.
Yet he is with us for all time. Alleluia!

Leader　　Lord Jesus,
the fullness of your love
fills the universe in all its parts.
Send your Spirit
to bless this table
and fill us with your life,
for ever and ever.

ALL　　Amen.

AFTER THE MEAL

Leader　　Lord Jesus,
true life of all,
we await the day
when you will come again.
Prepare us for the glory
which will be ours
in union with you,
for ever and ever.

ALL　　Amen.

PRATER 3

PRAYER **3**

BEFORE THE MEAL

Leader   At last God has made his dwelling among us.
             The old order has passed away.
             For behold, Jesus died
             and now lives for evermore. Alleluia!

      ALL   He has gone before us.
             Yet he is with us for all time. Alleluia!

Leader   Lord Jesus,
             whose Spirit dwells within us,
             be with us at this table.
             Nourish us for the kingdom
             where you are the First and the Last
             and the living One,
             for ever and ever.

      ALL   Amen.

AFTER THE MEAL

Leader   You are blest, Lord Jesus,
             and blest is your holy name.
             Through your Spirit
             you make all things new.
             To you belongs all time
             and all the ages,
             for ever and ever.

      ALL   Amen.

BEFORE THE MEAL

Leader   We have been brought into one body
by baptism in the one Spirit,
and that one Holy Spirit
was poured out for us to drink.
Behold, Jesus died
and now lives for evermore. Alleluia!

ALL   He has gone before us.
Yet he is with us for all time. Alleluia!

Leader   Lord Jesus,
in your love,
bless this table
and unite us more closely to you.
We make this prayer
gathered in your Spirit,
both now and for ever.

ALL   Amen.

AFTER THE MEAL

Leader   Lord God,
we thank you for this meal
and praise you for the gift of your Spirit,
who takes our life
and the inmost thoughts of our hearts
and transforms us into
the likeness of your Son,
who lives and reigns,
for ever and ever.

ALL   Amen.

Ordinary Time II

These prayers are used during the weeks following Pentecost Sunday until the First Sunday of Advent.

PRAYER 1

BEFORE THE MEAL

Leader   Blessed is the Lord, our God,
           Creator of the universe;
           for he provides nourishing food
           for all his creatures
           and sustains the whole world
           with his goodness, kindness, and loving favor.

   ALL   Give thanks to the Lord, for he is good,
           for his mercy endures for ever.

Leader   All-merciful God,
           send your life-giving Spirit
           on our household
           and on all dear to us,
           and bless this table
           as we join together and say:

   ALL   Amen.

AFTER THE MEAL

Leader   Give us grateful hearts, our Father,
           for all your mercies,
           and make us mindful of the needs of others,
           through Jesus Christ our Lord.

   ALL   Amen.

PRAYER **2**

BEFORE THE MEAL

Leader   God himself calls us
to share in the life of his Son,
Jesus Christ the Lord.
In this is our hope secured,
for Jesus lives to bring us
the Father's goodness, kindness, and loving favor.

ALL   Give thanks to the Lord, for he is good,
for his mercy endures for ever.

Leader   Ever-faithful God,
bless the food we are about to eat
and unite us in mind and heart
to your Son,
Jesus Christ, the Lord.

ALL   Amen.

AFTER THE MEAL

Leader   God our strength,
we thank you for food,
life,
and the enduring hope
that you share with us
through Jesus Christ our Lord.

ALL   Amen.

BEFORE THE MEAL

Leader   There is nothing in death or life,
nothing in all creation
that can separate us from the love of God
in Christ Jesus our Lord.
For, to this day, he sustains us
with his goodness, kindness, and loving favor.

ALL   Give thanks to the Lord, for he is good,
for his mercy endures for ever.

Leader   All-loving God,
bless this table
and through the work of your Spirit
shape us into the likeness of your Son,
Jesus Christ, the Lord.

ALL   Amen.

AFTER THE MEAL

Leader   Source, Guide, and Goal of all that is –
to you, Lord,
be praise and thanksgiving,
both now and for ever.

ALL   Amen.

PRAYER 4

BEFORE THE MEAL

Leader How great is the hope to which God calls us,
how tremendous the power
available to us who trust in him!
For God's Holy Spirit abides with us,
and fills us
with his goodness, kindness, and loving favor.

ALL Give thanks to the Lord, for he is good,
for his mercy endures for ever.

Leader Great and generous God,
nourish us in this meal.
Strengthen our hidden selves,
that through faith
Christ may dwell in our hearts
in love
both now and for ever.

ALL Amen.

AFTER THE MEAL

Leader Searcher of minds and hearts,
your power, working in us,
does infinitely more
than we dare to ask or imagine.
To you be glory and honor
in the Church
and in Christ Jesus
for ever and ever.

ALL Amen.